anythink

LIGHTNING
BOLT
BOOKS™

Cool Classic Cars

Jon M. Fishman

Lerner Publications ◆ Minneapolis

Lerner Publications Company
A division of Lerner Publishing Group, Inc.
241 First Avenue North
Minneapolis, MN 55401 USA

For reading levels and more information, look up this title at www.lernerbooks.com.

Library of Congress Cataloging-in-Publication Data

Names: Fishman, Jon M., author.
Title: Cool classic cars / Jon M. Fishman.
Description: Minneapolis : Lerner Publications, [2019] | Series: Lightning bolt books. Awesome rides | Includes bibliographical references and index.
Identifiers: LCCN 2017038557| ISBN 9781541519961 (lb : alk. paper) | ISBN 9781541527522 (pb : alk. paper)
Subjects: LCSH: Antique and classic cars—Juvenile literature.
Classification: LCC TL147 .F48 2019 | DDC 629.222—dc23

LC record available at https://lccn.loc.gov/2017038557

Manufactured in the United States of America
1-44332-34578-12/6/2017

Table of Contents

It's a Classic Car!

Honk! Honk! A classic car pulls up to the curb on the side of a street. The owner polished the car before taking it for a drive. It shines brightly in the sun.

Classic cars are old cars. Carmakers no longer build them. Some classic cars are more than one hundred years old!

This car is around one hundred years old. The company that made the car closed in 1938.

Some classic cars are rare. Only a few of them were ever built. Other classic cars are common. Factories made many of them for people to buy.

By 1930, Chevrolet was making almost one million vehicles each year. Chevrolet continues to be a very popular car company.

People enjoy classic cars for many reasons. The cars bring back happy memories for some people. Other people see the cars as beautiful works of art.

The Classic Car Story

In 1913, carmaker Henry Ford started building cars using an assembly line. His factory could make many cars in a short time.

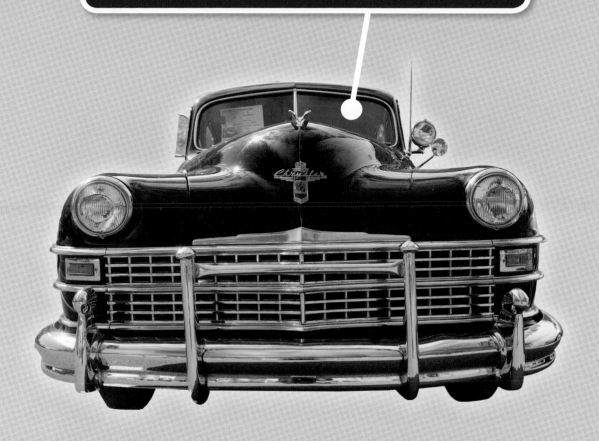

Chrysler still makes cars, but the last Packard car was built in 1956.

Soon other people began making cars this way. Companies such as Chrysler and Packard built popular vehicles. Many cars made between 1913 and 1950 became classic cars.

People began collecting classic cars in the late 1940s. Collectors made sure the cars would remain after factories stopped making them.

In the 1950s, classic car clubs printed magazines about their cars. They held shows and went on tours to show off their cars. People have been collecting classic cars ever since.

Classic Car Parts

Classic cars look like older types of modern cars you see on the road. Classic cars have four doors or two doors.

Classic cars were built to move people around in comfort. They have soft seats and plenty of room inside.

Some classic cars are convertibles. The wind blows across your face as you roll down the street. Hold onto your hat!

Classic cars may have an extra tire on the car's side. Others have large tail fins in the back. Some parts of classic cars are even made of wood!

Early tires were not very strong, so drivers had to replace flat tires often. Most cars had an extra tire on the side or back.

Classic Cars in Action

Bang! Bang! A collector pounds a dent out of a classic car. She is making the car look as it did when the car was brand new.

Judges at car events give collectors awards for how their cars run and look.

Collectors show off their cars in parades and special events. Classic car fans travel to shows around the world. The cars remind people of history.

People trade stories about their cars at classic car shows. They buy rare car parts and learn about ways to make their cars look like new.

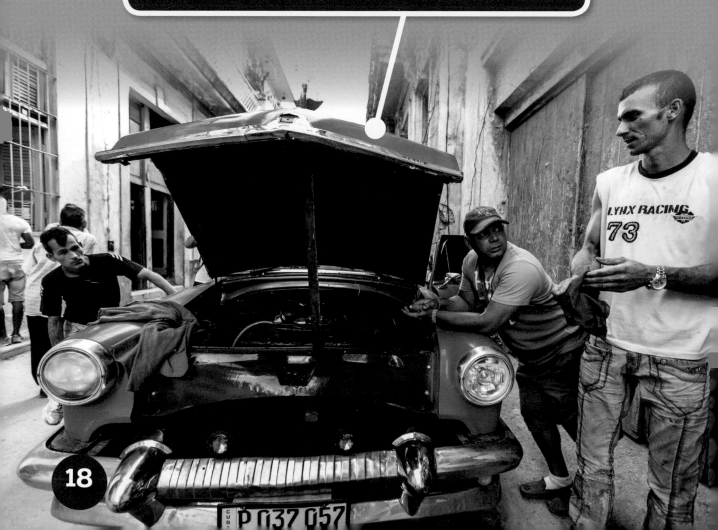

Collectors look for old car parts like the ones originally used in their cars.

As time goes by, cars built
before 1950 will become more
and more rare. But carmakers
are building new cars all the
time. Someday new cars
may become classics too!

Classic Car Diagram

hood

tire

extra
tire

door

Classic Car Facts

- The first cars were called horseless carriages. A carriage is a vehicle with four wheels that is pulled by a horse.

- The first car built on Henry Ford's assembly line was called the Model T. By 1925, a new Model T cost about $300.

- In 2017, a Mercedes-Benz 540K Special Roadster sold for $6.6 million! Only about twenty-five of these classic cars were made.

Glossary

assembly line: machines and people in a factory that make a product over and over again

collector: a person who gathers things such as cars or stamps

convertible: a car with a roof that folds back

factory: a building where products are built

polish: to make something shiny by rubbing it

tour: a journey that stops in different places

vehicle: an object used to move people or things

Further Reading

Boothroyd, Jennifer. *From the Model T to Hybrid Cars: How Transportation Has Changed*. Minneapolis: Lerner Publications, 2012.

Burgan, Michael. *Who Was Henry Ford?* New York: Grosset & Dunlap, 2014.

Car Facts for Kids
http://www.sciencekids.co.nz/sciencefacts/vehicles/cars.html

Facts about Cars
http://www.scienceforkidsclub.com/cars.html

How Do Engines Work?
http://www.brainson.org/how-do-engines-work-road-trip-pt-1

Mara, Wil. *Henry Ford: Automotive Innovator*. New York: Children's Press, 2018.

Index

Photo Acknowledgments

The images in this book are used with the permission of: filmfoto/iStock Editorial/Getty Images, p. 2; Sjoerd van der Wal/iStock Unreleased/Getty Images Plus/Getty Images, pp. 4, 5; LordRunar/iStock/Getty Images Plus/Getty Images, p. 6; filmfoto/iStock Editorial/Getty Images Plus/Getty Images, p. 7; Darren Brode/Shutterstock.com, p. 7; Science History Images/Alamy Stock Photo, p. 8; marcduf/iStock Unreleased/Getty Images, p. 9; Peter Dazeley/The Image Bank/Getty Images, p. 10; Mariusz S. Jurgielewicz/Shutterstock.com, p. 11; Margo Harrison/Shutterstock.com, p. 12; JuergenBosse/iStock Unreleased/Getty Images, p. 13; Charlie Edward/Shutterstock.com, p. 14; caia image/Alamy Stock Photo, p. 16; Leena Robinson/Shutterstock.com, p. 17; Atlantide Phototravel/Corbis Documentary/Getty Images, p. 18; Alex Neshitoff/Shutterstock.com, p. 19; Margo Harrison/Shutterstock.com, p. 20; Burachet/Shutterstock.com, p. 22.

Front cover: Martin Charles Hatch/Shutterstock.com.

Main body text set in Billy Infant regular 28/36. Typeface provided by SparkType.